The LITTLE

Picasso

Catherine de Duve

Discover the world of the famous Spanish painter

KATE'ART
EDITIONS

PICASSO'S

It's the turn of the century. Culture and art are flourishing in France, and the industrial revolution is in full swing. There's a lot of building going on, the city's becoming bigger and better all the time! These new building projects include the Grand Palais, the Gare d'Orsay station and the Alexander III Bridge...

Paris is hosting the 1900 Universal Exhibition. Each country has its own picturesque pavilion, where it displays its scientific achievements, inventions, culture and art.

Picasso is 19, and one of his pictures has been chosen for the Spanish pavilion. He is going to Paris for the first time! What will he see there?

At the foot of the Eiffel Tower is a huge "celestial globe", which the public are in awe of.

The Lumière brothers project a film onto a huge screen for the very first time...

The "Palace of Electricity" is lit up with electric lighting, which is becoming increasingly common in homes, streets, factories and railways. The world is changing!

Paris's first underground Metro line is now open. The entrances to the stations have been designed by Hector Guimard in Art Nouveau style.

The French empire has colonies in Africa and the Caribbean. African objects, masks and statues are brought back to museums in Paris to be studied and admired by the French public.

PABLO PICASSO

Pablo Ruiz Picasso is born on the 25th of October 1881 in Malaga, Spain. His father is a decorator and painter, as well as an art teacher, and his mother comes from Andalusia. Pablo has two little sisters, Dolores and Conchita. His dad teaches him to paint at a very early age and he creates his first proper pictures at the age of 8. He is very gifted!

He enrols in the School of Fine Arts where his father teaches, then in the Academy of Barcelona, when the family moves there. But he finds it all so boring. He rents his own studio before leaving to study in Madrid.

Picasso is 15 years old when he exhibits this academic-style painting "The First Communion". His talent is recognised early on and he receives a gold medal for it.

In 1900, the young Spanish painter arrives in Paris for the first time! Picasso explores the Universal Exhibition. The next year he settles in Montmartre with his friend Casegemas. He discovers the art of Cézanne*, Degas*, Bonnard and especially Toulouse-Lautrec, whose paintings fascinate him.

Toulouse-Lautrec

Degas

Here are the painters whose work Picasso first sees in Paris. What sort of things do they paint?

Cézanne

* *To find out more, take a look at* The Little Cézanne *and* The Little Degas *in the same series.*

5

Back in Barcelona, Picasso paints more than 50 pictures in just over a year. The colour blue is everywhere in his paintings! It expresses his sadness: his friend Casegemas, who stayed behind in Paris, has tragically just taken his own life. Picasso is devastated…

In Paris, the young Spanish painter exhibits at the gallery of the art dealer Ambroise Vollard. The exhibition is a great success! Fifteen pictures have been sold before the exhibition even opens. He signs the paintings "Picasso", his mother's surname.

What name would you choose for yourself if you were an artist? Create your artist's signature below.

In 1903 Picasso paints a poor family at the seaside. Can you see the beach and the waves? The people look sad and alone. Picasso paints their bodies longer than they would be naturally, in the "mannerist" style of the painter El Greco, who he admires greatly. This is the beginning of his "blue period".

El Greco
1541-1614

How does this picture make you feel?

ROSE PERIOD

In 1904, Picasso moves to Paris. He rents a studio in the Bateau-Lavoir area, where other artists, including Van Dongen, Gris, Brancusi, Modigliani and Max Jacob, are also living. There he also meets Fernande Olivier, his first love. Picasso visits the Autumn Salon of 1905, where he first comes across the paintings of Rousseau*, Cézanne*, Manet* and Matisse*, which are causing quite a scandal!

Picasso and his friends often go to the Le Lapin Agile ("The Nimble Rabbit") cabaret, as unusually the owner accepts drawings as payment. From his studio, he can see the big top of the Medrano Circus. Picasso likes to paint the harlequins, animal tamers, clowns and acrobats. Vollard buys most of his work and at last Picasso no longer needs to worry about money.

 Draw something from your own Rose period.

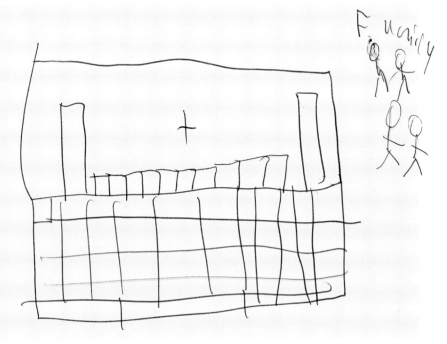

* *To find out more, take a look at* The Little Manet, The Little Rousseau, The Little Cézanne *and* The Little Matisse *in the same series.*

8

Who are these people in costumes? A family of acrobats are talking in the middle of a desert. What are they saying to each other? They look like characters from old paintings! Although there are several of them, the atmosphere is one of sadness and loneliness. The blue of the sky gradually fades from the picture, leaving pinkish-brown colours. This is the beginning of Picasso's Rose period.

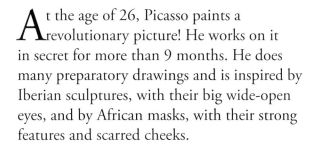

At the age of 26, Picasso paints a revolutionary picture! He works on it in secret for more than 9 months. He does many preparatory drawings and is inspired by Iberian sculptures, with their big wide-open eyes, and by African masks, with their strong features and scarred cheeks.

Iberian: *coming from the ancient civilisation of the Iberian Peninsula – Spain and Portugal.*

Here are the young ladies of Avignon. Where are they? One of them is holding open a scarlet stage curtain. Behind them are the folds of a heavy blue and white drape. Brrr… it looks freezing, like an iceberg! They are looking at us strangely… Their bulging eyes stare right at us. What large noses they have! All the women are shown in profile, "so that people can see their noses", says Picasso. "One day, no one will think that they look at all wrong!" Their bodies are very angular, not at all delicate or flattering. Picasso doesn't want to show his figures in just one position.

Who can we see from the side, the front and behind, all at the same time?

How many people can you see? Find the lady crouching down, the curtain, the *still* life and the faces inspired by African masks.

CUBISM

One day the painter George Braque pays a visit to Picasso's studio. When he sees the *Young Ladies of Avignon*, he exclaims that "it's as if someone had drunk petrol and was breathing out fire!"

The two artists work together to develop a style that would come to be known as *Cubism*. They are inspired by Paul Cézanne* who paints using small cubic shapes, opening up a new dimension in painting.

As if he were creating a puzzle, Picasso breaks up landscape, portrait and still life paintings into little pieces. These fragments, suggesting more than one viewpoint, are then rearranged on a background of grey and brown. This style is known as **Analytical Cubism** (1908-1912).

Find these details in the painting:

Hair

Noses

Bottles

Hands

Chains

Buttons

* *To find out more, take a look at* The Little Matisse, *p.15 and* The Little Cézanne, *pp. 28-29 in the same series.*

The word "*Cubism*" comes from the Fauve painter Henri Matisse*, who speaks of "little cubes", and from the art critic Louis Vauxcelles who writes an article in November 1908, reviewing the Braque exhibition, in which he states that "Mr Braque is not interested in form, and reduces everything to cubes."

In 1910, Picasso paints the art dealer Kahnweiler. Can you see him in this picture?

GUITAR

In the summer of 1910, Picasso goes painting with his friend Derain, in Cadaquès, Spain. He paints ten new pictures. Here is the guitar-player with his guitar. Can you see them? They are made up of lines and angles. Can you hear the strumming rhythm of the guitar? What is he playing? The guitarist's head has become a cylinder. Where is the rest of his body?

Find the guitar in the picture.

The next year, Picasso meets Eva Gouel. He calls her by a nickname, which he sings happily to himself. What name is that? In this picture, a woman sings along to a popular song *Ma Jolie* ("my pretty one"). Could it be Eva?

There are lines, fragments of picture and diagonals all over the place. It's so confusing! This is almost an abstract painting. But there are still some traces of his subject in the picture.

Find the woman, 4 fingers, guitar strings, Eva's nickname, and the treble clef.

COLLAGE

Braque is exploring a new technique. He used to be a house painter, and stencils letters onto his paintings, uses a comb to imitate wood, and sticks sand or bits of paper onto the canvas. He's invented the collage!

Create a still life in the style of Braque and Picasso. Like them, arrange your objects artistically. Don't forget to stick something real onto your picture!

Now Picasso has an idea! Onto the canvas he sticks a real piece of oilcloth, looking like the caning on a chair. What a surprising effect! He's added a piece of real life to his picture. It's never been done before! In fact, why imitate a paintbrush when you can stick one onto the canvas?

Picasso wants to make his pictures real again. He creates the atmosphere of a bar by using the sort of false wood used for café tables, and by stencilling on letters and numbers which look like newspaper print.

True or false? Look at these objects, and try and see which are real and which are painted: the lemon, the glass, the pipe, the string, the newspaper and the oilcloth. What is the frame made of?

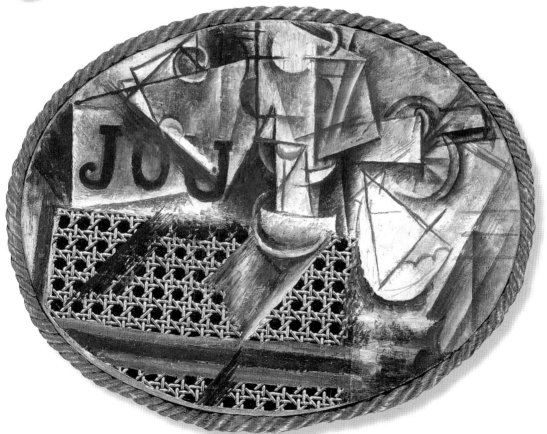

After these collages Picasso starts painting again. He now paints objects as if they were stuck onto the canvas. He's imitating something which itself is imitating reality. He's playing with ideas and turning art on its head! This is the second stage of Cubism, **Synthetic Cubism** (1912-1919).

Look at this Harlequin. Is this a collage or a painting?

The next year, Braque and Picasso exhibit their work in New York, but World War I breaks out and their partnership has to come to an end. In August 1914 Braque is called up to fight in the army, but Picasso, as he is Spanish, can carry on painting. He returns to a more classical style, like that of his Rose period. He draws inspiration from the *Comedia dell'Arte* (popular 17th century Italian theatre), when he draws Harlequin and Pierrot.

Who are these three masked figures? Find Pierrot the clown playing the clarinet, Harlequin strumming his guitar, the monk holding the music and the dog.

DANCER

In 1917, Picasso joins the Ballets Russes and the troop's impresario Serge Diaghilev in Rome. He designs the costumes and set for their ballet *Parade*, as well as the stage curtain. He meets the composer Igor Stravinsky and a Russian dancer, Olga Koklova, who he will go on to marry in 1918.

In Italy, Picasso visits Rome, Naples, Pompeii... and discovers the ancient world. He paints statuesque women like those in antique frescoes.

Picasso is from the Mediterranean, and likes to spend his holidays by the sea. Here are two giant-like women, draped in Greek or Roman gowns, solid as statues and supple as dancers, running along the beach. Could one of them be Olga, pregnant? Their son Paolo is born in 1921.

Look at the painting. Can you see the dancers? How many of them are there? Can you see them dancing? Think of a name for their dance. Where are they?

The summer of 1925 is a very difficult time. Picasso and Olga separate. His art becomes more aggressive. In the same year, Picasso displays his work at the first Surrealist exhibition in Paris, which marks the beginning of a new art movement*.

* To find out more, see The Little Magritte in the same series, pp. 10-11

GUERNICA

In April 1937, Civil War is tearing Spain apart. The small town of Guernica, in the Basque Country, is bombed by German Nazi warplanes at the request of General Franco. Picasso is horrified and wants to depict the terror of war and the suffering of his people. He uses a range of greys, and paints the violence like that of a bullfight. Can you see the bullfighter lying on the ground, the dying horse and the bull, the victor?

Find these details in the painting:

The Horse: the Spanish nation, suffering and struggling.
The Lamp and the Light Bulb: human reason, which seems to have been lost.
The Bull: the brutal violence inflicted by the enemy forces.
The Bullfighter: a symbol of Spain, mortally wounded.

 The Spanish Civil War: this lasted from 1936 to 1939, as Spaniards fought Spaniards in their own country. On one side were the Nationalists, and on the other the Republicans. The war ended with the victory of the fascist dictator General Francisco Franco.

MAYA

Picasso has several people he can regularly paint. They are the source of his inspiration. He has four children: Paul, Maya, Paloma and Claude. He loves painting them, and wants to paint spontaneously again, like a child! He is inspired by children's drawings, and tries to paint in the same way, freely and without having to stick to any rules. The results are fresh and new!

When I was eight, I painted like Raphael. It has taken me a whole lifetime to learn to paint like a child.

What is little Maya playing with? She is the daughter of Picasso and Marie-Thérèse Walter. Picasso changes the shape of her face, showing it from the front and the side at the same time. But it still looks like her...

Find Maya's toys. How old is she? How does she wear her hair?

ANIMALS

Picasso is into everything! He likes making sculptures out of old bits and pieces, sometimes fished out of dustbins. He uses the objects he finds to make an animal's head. What can he make out of a bicycle saddle and an old pair of handlebars?

Can you see an animal taking shape?

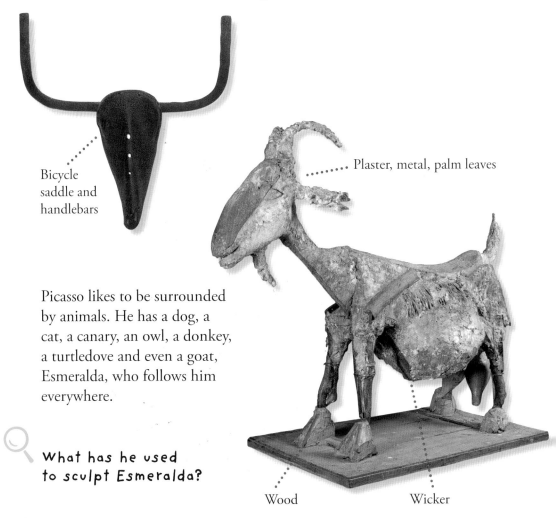

Bicycle saddle and handlebars

Plaster, metal, palm leaves

Picasso likes to be surrounded by animals. He has a dog, a cat, a canary, an owl, a donkey, a turtledove and even a goat, Esmeralda, who follows him everywhere.

What has he used to sculpt Esmeralda?

Wood

Wicker

In 1948, Picasso moves to Vallauris.
He makes ceramics, plates, dishes and vases.

Turn this plate into a work of art, as Picasso
would have done.

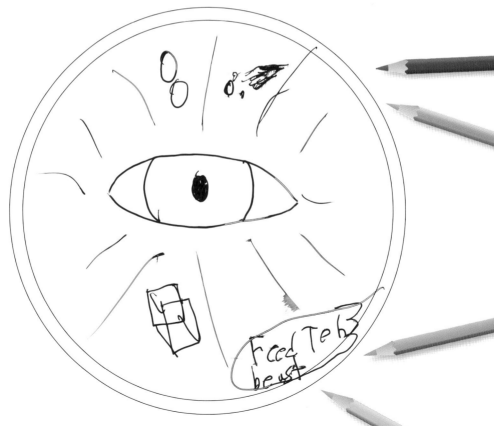

PICASSO

Since he was a child, Picasso has been fascinated by the great painters of the past. At the age of 14, he visits the Prado museum in Madrid with his father. There for the first time he sees pictures by the painter *Diego Velázquez*. Years later, in 1957, Picasso spends four months at home, hardly going out, studying the work of this Spanish painter. For Picasso, Velázquez is the greatest painter of all.

Diego Velázquez *(1599-1660) was the court painter of the Spanish King Philip IV. He is considered to be one of the greatest Spanish painters ever.*

Compare the two pictures. One was painted three hundred years after the other! Which one do you prefer?

VELÁZQUEZ

MATADOR

At the end of his life, Picasso feels nostalgic for the country where he was born. His mind keeps wandering back to great figures from Spanish history and culture: conquistadors and musketeers, wearing capes, boots and feathered hats. They are swashbuckling heroes but look funny too!

Picasso paints several bullfighting scenes. They remind him of his childhood. Here is the proud matador, the chief bullfighter. He is the one who flourishes the red cape in front of the bull in the arena, and finally puts it to death.

 Find the various parts of the matador's costume.

30

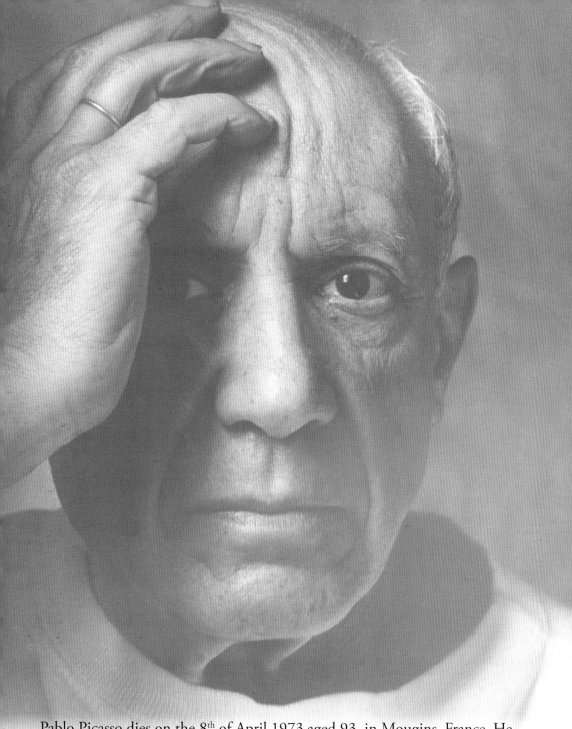

Pablo Picasso dies on the 8th of April 1973 aged 93, in Mougins, France. He is now recognised as one of the greatest artists of the twentieth century.

Text: Catherine de Duve
Contributions from: Aurore t'Kint, Isabelle Gérard and Véronique Lux
Concept and Production: Kate'Art Editions
Translation from the French: Rachel Cowler

PHOTOGRAPHY CREDITS:

Pablo Picasso: Paris: Musée Picasso: *She-Goat (Esmeralda)*, 1950: cover, p. 10, p. 23, p. 26 - *Still-Life with Chair Caning*, 1912: p. 16 (detail), p. 17- *Two Women Running on the Beach*, 1922: p. 20 - *Bull's Head, leather saddle and metal handlebars*, 1943: p. 26 - *Spanish Plate*, 1957: p. 27 - *The Matador*, 1971: p. 30 | Centre Georges Pompidou, Musée national d'art moderne: *The Guitarist*, 1910: p. 14 | **Madrid:** Museo Nacional Centro de Arte Reina Sofia: *Guernica*, 1937: cover, pp.22-23| **Barcelona:** Museo Picasso: *First Communion*, 1895-1896: p. 4 - *Las Méninas, after Velázquez*, 1957: p. 28, p. 29 (details)| **Washington, D.C.:** National Gallery of Art: *The Tragedy*, 1903: p. 7 - *The Acrobats (The Family of Saltimbanques)*, 1905: p. 9 | **New York:** Museum of Modern Art (MoMA): *The Young Ladies of Avignon*, 1907: cover, p. 10 (details), p. 11, p. 12 - *Guitar*, 1914: cover, p. 14 - *Ma Jolie*, 1911-1912: p. 15 - *Harlequin*, 1915: cover, p. 18 - *Three Musicians*, 1921: cover, p. 19 | **London:** Tate Modern: *Three Dancers*, 1925: p. 21 | **Lucerne:** Collection Rosengart: *Girl with a Boat (Maya Picasso)*, 1938: cover (details), p. 24 (details), p. 25 | **Prague:** Narodni Galerie: *Self-portrait*, 1907: p. 1, p. 4 | **Chicago:** Art Institute: *Portrait of D.H. Kanhweiler*, 1910.: p. 12 (details), p. 13 | **Private collection:** *Ceramic plate, decorated with goat's head in profile*, 1950: p. 27- *Anthropomorphic Vase*, 1952: p. 27

Photography: *Picasso in Paris*, 1904: p. 2, p. 5 - *Picasso painting*: p. 27 - ©Arnold Newman: *Picasso, Vallauris*, 1957: p. 31

© succession Picasso – SABAM Belgium 2014

Others: Paris: Musée d'Orsay: Cézanne: *The Card Players*, 1890: p. 5 - Degas: *Harlequin and Colombine*, c.1886-1890: Velázquez: **Madrid:** Museo Nacional del Prado: *Las Meninas*, 1656: p. 29 | El Greco: **Toledo:** Museo Del Greco: *Saint James the Greater*, c.1610-1614: p. 7 | Toulouse-Lautrec: **Private collection:** *Moulin Rouge poster, The Glutton*, 1891: p. 5 | **Archives:** *Le Grand Palais*, c.1900: p. 2 – *The Lumiere Brothers: Auguste (1862-1954) et Louis (1864-1948)*: p .2 - *The Eiffel Tower and the Celestial Globe at the 1900 Universal Exhibition in Paris*: p. 2 – *"The Palace of Electricity"*, 1900: p. 3 – *The Metropolitan, Paris*, c.1900: p. 3 - © Nimbus: *African Mask, Punu, Gabon*: p. 3

With thanks to: Christine Pinault, Picasso Administration, Aurore t'Kint, Isabelle Gérard, Véronique Lux, Stuart Forward, Daniel de Duve and all those who contributed to the creation of this book.

All works of Kate'Art Editions are available in French & English with many titles available in Dutch, Spanish, German, Russian, Japanese and Danish.

Visit us online: www.kateart.com